BETWEEN SHADOWS & SUNLIGHT

A Journey of Love, Growth, and Self-Discovery

WRITTEN BY

SRAVANTHI TANAKALLU

ISBN
Hardcase 979-8-89744-606-3
Paperback 979-8-89724-573-4

Contents

Contents

Contents

Author

Sravanthi Tanakallu, from Madanapalle, Andhra Pradesh, holds a postgraduate degree in Management and is passionate about social service. She currently works on girls' education in Bangalore. A Mandala artist, solo traveler, and avid reader of Psychology and Spirituality, Sravanthi practices yoga and Vipassana meditation to nurture her well-being.

Her travels and volunteer work have introduced her to diverse people and experiences that continue to shape her journey. Beginning her path of self-discovery in Rishikesh, she embraces the balance between the shadows and sunlight of life.

Writing became a source of happiness and relief, offering solace in both joyful and difficult times. Through her words, Sravanthi invites others to explore their own journeys of self-discovery and healing.

She can be contacted through email: sravanthit89@gmail.com

Illustrator

Praveena Prathap Menon, hailing from Palakkad, Kerala, the illustrator is a student of journalism and psychology. She is passionate about photography and various forms of art, with a specialty in Mural painting, Digital art, and Illustrations. She has also embarked on a spiritual journey and practices Yoga.

Preface

Life is a journey between shadows and sunlight—a mix of challenges and joys, struggles and hope. This book, *Between Shadows and Sunlight*, is a reflection of that journey.

This book is not just a collection of words—it is a journey of growth, healing, and self-discovery. It is an ode to the moments that break us and the ones that make us whole again. It is a celebration of the people who walk with us, those who leave us, and those who teach us lessons we never knew we needed.

The shadows taught me resilience, while the sunlight reminded me of the beauty in new beginnings. Both have shaped who I am today.

As you read through these pages, I hope you find a reflection of your own journey. May it inspire you to embrace the shadows as much as the sunlight, to seek meaning in every experience, and to cherish the magic of this extraordinary life.

Welcome to Between Shadows and Sunlight. I hope it touches your heart and brings you comfort and hope.

Acknowledgments

First and foremost, I want to thank my parents, Sujatha Tanakallu and Nagaraja Tanakallu. I owe everything to them. Your love, sacrifices, and unwavering support has shaped my journey, and for that, I am forever grateful and deeply indebted. To my brother, Sreenath Tanakallu, who stood by my side with silent strength and unconditional love—thank you for being my constant.

I truly want to thank all my teachers, mentors, and spiritual gurus who have taught me, shared their wisdom, and helped me become a better person.

I want to extend my heartfelt thanks to my extended family—my grandparents, aunts, uncles, and cousins. Your encouragement and support have been the foundation upon which I have built my life.

I also want to express my deepest gratitude to my dearest friend, Kinnera V. Your unconditional love has been a gift beyond measure. Through you, I experienced pure love and understanding that has been a seed for my growth. Thank you for the confidence you had on me when I was not as confident and for accepting me for who I was.

Thank you to all my friends who have been my constant support and pillars of strength throughout this journey.

You have been there for me through thick and thin, and I am deeply grateful for your presence and encouragement. Your friendship has been a source of joy, and I couldn't have done this without you.

I want to acknowledge the support I have received from my friends, Bhawna Dwivedi Mandloi and Shwetha Narayanan, who offered their time to read the manuscript and helped with proofreading. I also want to thank Praveena Prathap Menon, the illustrator of this book.

And to everyone who has loved me, left me, or doubted my worth—thank you from the depths of my heart. Each of you played a unique role in my life, offering lessons and experiences that helped me grow, discover myself, and seek meaning beyond the surface. I wouldn't have evolved into the person I am today without your presence, however brief it may have been.

To the universe, thank you for every experience—both the blessings and the challenges. With each passing day, I am beginning to understand your magic, your protection, and your infinite wisdom. As I write these words, my heart overflows with love and gratitude for everything I've received—and even for what I haven't. Words fall short, and tears of joy express what I cannot.

Thank you for shaping this journey between shadows and sunlight.

Love

Sravanthi Tanakallu

Sunset Saga!

In the embrace of his arms,
Love flows in waves,
Sunset hues kissing the ocean in the most gentlest of
ways.
Saying a short goodbye,
Only to meet tomorrow,
A silent promise,
A gentle affair to witness,
And so I stood in silence,
While the Waves touched my feet.
I became a part of an intimate moment,
A sense of warmth and a connection felt so deep,
This Long-distance is a bittersweet!
But True beauty is in the wait,
With a hopeful tomorrow,
Love blossoms again,
Painting the skies in pink,
A sign of arrival!
Beyond beautiful and calming,
That's the love I witnessed,
That's the love I embrace!

Perfect Moment!

Lying under the sky,
Slight breeze making it a chilly night,
Gazing at thousands of stars,
Some soothing music playing along.
My soul is dancing!
It felt like the perfect moment,
Until I remembered you,
Then I started to wonder, what you must be doing?
Miles apart!
But strangely it didn't feel any longer,
Felt comfort knowing that we both live under the same
sky,
Somewhere happy,
Somewhere safe,
Once again, my soul caught the beat around to dance,
And I returned to my dreamland!

Sravanthi Tanakallu

Love is Love

Love is love,
Not bound by gender,
Religion, caste, or community,
Not by ethnicity.
Love is love,
Not confined by rules,
Not by beliefs,
Traditions, norms,
Or regulations.
Love is love,
Unbounded,
Simple and pure,
Beautiful and true.
How can anyone define who loves,
Or how love should be,
And what love is even?
Our love can be selfish,
Immature, and foolish,
It's unfair to LOVE,
Which is meant to be bigger,
More profound than we know,
Feel or understand.

So Let love be!
Flowing like magic,
Selfless,
Beyond any logic,
A blissful feeling,
Beyond any imagination.
So let love live,
In its true sense,
Free from definitions,
And meaningless constraints.

•••

Sravanthi Tanakallu

Feel the Magic Around

I asked you to show me your world,
But you showed me the soul of it,
How can I ever explain this feeling?
And how beautiful it is!
For the first time, I have no words.
I don't think I could explain it;
No word could do justice.
And so, I simply let it be,
Enjoyed the silence,
And felt the magic around.

Conversations Between Heart & Mind

In the quiet of the night,
Heart and Mind begin their fight.

Heart says, "I love you"
Mind replies, "Let go, be wise"
Think of what is best for you,
Not just dreams that might fall through."

Heart beats loud, saying "I know the power of love
Trust in me,
Feel the warmth of love."

Mind stays clear and logical, saying, "avoid the tear.
In this world so mean and cold,
Let wisdom guide your mind, not love
And It's best to be cautious."

Logic may guide the path ahead,
But love is the light of life.
"Is it logical?" Mind debates,
Weighing pros and cons, assessing fates.

Yet Heart whispers, "It's always right,
For love alone is true and real."
In the end,
Will they ever stop debating?
And exist peacefully together!

Sravanthi Tanakallu

What is Love?

What is love, after all?
Is it a feeling or a state of being?
An emotion or a choice?
A thought or an unconscious pull toward someone?
But what if none of that truly matters?
What if love, whatever it is, simply needs to happen?

I want to love fiercely, fearlessly, and purely—
The way I want to.
A love that's raw, real, and unapologetically authentic.
I don't need love to be perfect,
Because perfect is honestly boring.
I want love to be a little messy, a little chaotic, and a little
confused—
But undeniably genuine.

I don't need us to have everything figured out.
Because what's left to discover,
If we've already unraveled every mystery.
I want us to build, to stumble, to celebrate small victories,
And to find joy in growing together.

I don't want us to share every interest,
Because I'd rather learn yours,

See the world through your eyes,
And find beauty in your perspective as well.

Perhaps not everyone will understand the way I love—
And that's okay.
Let them stay confused,
Too afraid to fall, too scared to lose themselves,
Yet yearning for something real.
But I know this:
I don't need my love to be understood or approved.

Love was never meant to be hidden or withheld.
If you love someone, let them know.
Don't hold them back—
Let them go, let them explore, let them fly.
And if you can, be their wings.
After all, we all have numbered days
If you don't take chances, embrace failure,
How will you ever learn, grow, or truly live?
I want to create memories with those I love.
To gather stories—wild, beautiful, messy stories—
So one day, I can look back and cherish the life I've lived.

PS: What is love to you?

•••

Your Thoughts are Fading Away

While we don't talk anymore,
I wrote a thousand letters in my head.
Waiting, praying and hoping,
That you will somehow get all these messages,
And feeling disappointed
Watching moments pass by!
I wrote some more letters,
Until a moment came by,
Where I don't have any more
Thoughts left to write,
Tears left to cry.
But I felt a different pain-
A pain, that your thoughts are fading away!
And You became another memory,
Memories that come back,
Reminding me of your presence.
But I know one day,
Life will happen to both of us.
And I will not have those memories too,
So, the only thing that I do,
Until that happens,
And when I think of you is,

I smile,
With your face smiling back at me,
I pray,
That you shine through all the odds of life!
That you stay happy wherever you are!
That you stay happy wherever you are!!

• • •

One Day!

You are the last thread
between hope and despair!

I hope one day I realise
I am worthy
And not get consumed by someone else's opinion of me

Giving!

I wish I had learned to receive earlier.
All I knew was how to give, endlessly,
Until I was completely drained.
I never realised the importance of balance or questioned
why I equated goodness with giving.
I tried to unlearn, but I've come to accept that I'm a giver.
Now, I focus on protecting my energy and choosing wisely
whom I give to.

Reflections

How do you relate to the idea that love is both beautiful and painful, and how has this duality impacted your own experiences?

____

____

____

____

____

____

____

____

____

____

____

____

In what ways do you see the importance of self-love in the context of romantic relationships, and how does it influence your interactions with others?

____

____

____

____

____

____

____

____

____

____

____

____

How does the concept of love being free and unbound by societal norms resonate with your own beliefs and experiences?

____

____

____

____

____

____
____
____
____
____
____
____
____

What moments in your life have you felt a profound sense of connection, similar to the one described in ‹Perfect Moment!'?

____
____
____
____
____
____
____
____
____
____
____
____

How has love, in its various forms, contributed to your personal growth and resilience?

____

____

____

____

____

____

____

____

____

____

____

____

____

Can you think of a time when embracing the messiness and chaos of love led to a deeper understanding of yourself or others?

____

____

____

____

____

____

____

____

____

____

____

____

How do you balance the emotional and logical aspects of love in your relationships?

____

____

____

____

____

____

____

____

____

____

____

____

What insights have you gained about the healing process after losing someone you love, and how have you found peace and gratitude in such times?

____

____

____

____

____

____

____

____

____

____

____

____

____

What are some of your favourite lines from the 'Love' section?

____

____

____

____

____

____

Notes:

Growing

Sravanthi Tanakallu

Write Your Own Story

I will write my own story,
A beautiful one,
A story that my younger self will be in awe of,
And my older self will be proud and content with it.

Stories of All Kind

Some stories are beautiful, some are painful.

Some we remember, some we forget.

Some we cherish, some we dislike.

Some we share, some we don't.

Some teach us lessons, and some give us experience.

Every human being has a story to tell, and every story has something to offer.

This whole universe is made of innumerable stories, not atoms.

Lived a Thousand Lives

Right now, it is all chaos in my head, trying to escape, but I don't see a way.It's scares the shit out of me.
And then I sit with my thoughts-
A flood of thoughts, and me struggling to focus,
i reiterate whole situations in my head so to see what went wrong.
I overthink the multiple possibilities.
I try and try, but I don't see a way to stop them anymore.
I sometimes wonder how it would be to live in unawareness, and to have settled down like my parents asked me to.
Maybe I would have been happy and adjusted to living that way,
Then I think I would have never met this person that I'm becoming and could become.
It's a battle between what I was, and what I'm becoming.
Although I'm excited that it was a beautiful, bumpy, long journey, and I liked this version,
I'm excited about what more I would know about me
In all this, I have lived a thousand lives and can't wait for more,
To see different versions of me, each one better than the other.

I know with each breath that I take, I'm becoming a new me and also a step closer to death.
I feel I have less time and many new things to learn about myself
It's tiring sometimes with my complicated brain,
But I guess I need a better approach to handle,
Lot of patience, and strength to go through the old patterns.
I hope one day soon, I will gather my courage to handle this pain.
I have never known to handle this guilt and grief together,
Questions to which I don't have answers to.
Im learning to surrender slowly,
Trying to live in the moment, taking it slowly and moment by moment.

Sravanthi Tanakallu

Look within Yourself

This constant search for something.
I thought changing the external circumstances,
Could change mine
So I changed places, people, jobs and homes-
Giving an instant relief for sure.
A safe bubble!
An escape!
Something that felt easier.
But wait,
There they are again.
Waiting for you-
Same patterns and situations,
Until you learn to realise,
Nothing external could help!
So stay.
Breathe.
Look within yourself.
You will find a treasure,
A voice that does not have words.
But you know everything that you need to know,
Making you calmer and wiser.
So stay this time,
And look within yourself,
Silently and patiently!

Sravanthi Tanakallu

Choose Yourself First!

Years and years of tuning,
Doesn't matter what you like.
No conversations over your choices,
No discussions on how you feel.
You are taught to sacrifice
For your parents,
Then your partner,
And then your kids.
But you name it different
So to not feel guilty.
You will learn slowly but strongly,
To put everyone else first.
I thought that's love,
And that's how it should be.
But growing up,
It became messy.
Because I have put everyone else I know
Family, friendships and relationships.
I was happy doing it, just like I always knew.
Slowly, it started to feel overwhelming,
But still,
I struggle to unlearn it,
And put myself first.
I tried and tried but got tired.

It isn't easy.
But I have a hopeful heart
That one day,
I will put myself first,
Before anyone else.
Care for and love myself first.
It doesn't matter
What others approve of.
I will dress up the way my body feels comfortable,
Eat less or more until my tummy feels happy,
Sit the way my body feels relaxed,
Put my word if I have a point to make,
Laugh my heart out,
Define my life,
Decide my path,
And not anyone else!

•••

Sravanthi Tanakallu

Seeking

It was my choice
To question the rules,
To break the barriers,
To confront my fears,
To check on my beliefs,
To stand for what's beauty meant for me,
To stand for what I support,
To decide what kind of society that I want to be a part of.
I don't know if it's even the way to do anything,
But I know it definitely introduces me to a stronger version
of myself.
I would like to take all that is mine, and let go of things
that are not.
There was a sense of liberation,
A sense of completeness within me.
Feeling alive all over again.
I want to wake up to a better version of me.
Until then I would ponder upon different things that
would help me question, seek, and find out what I am
after all this-
To find myself while slowly breaking the strong
foundations of harmful beliefs and fears.

Sravanthi Tanakallu

Finding Answers in Silence

I never knew how to stop,
How to slow down.
Mind always rushed-
So much to learn,
So much to see.
Nothing to do?
My mind wanders
To do something.
Restlessness kicks in.
I find something so as to not pause,
Do something so as to feel productive.
Life has a way to teach.
If you don't stop, it will.
And so I paused for a while,
To connect,
To observe,
To learn,
To reflect,
To reset.
It hasn't been easy,
But I'm gradually learning
To be slow,
To be calm,

To be with myself,
To not think,
To not plan.
Some days I can't,
Some days I can,
But getting better at it,
Finding answers in silence!

Sravanthi Tanakallu

Another Breath - Another Chance at Living

Isn't it scary and painful?
You breathe now,
And the next moment you are not sure if you will be alive.
But why is it painful?
Is it the pain of knowing you are gonna die?
Or is it the pain of letting go of everything you have?
Or the physical pain that you can't bear?
When I die, I want to be ready.
How can I?
How can I let go of my dear life?
I guess I'm not ready to die yet.
Maybe no one will ever be!
We simply have to accept death
Because it is the only reality of our lives.
Learn to live, and so you learn to die.
There is so much to learn.
My soul needs this body.
So I guess it's not today.
I'm grateful for this life,
For another breath,
For another heartbeat,
For another sunrise,
And for another chance at living.

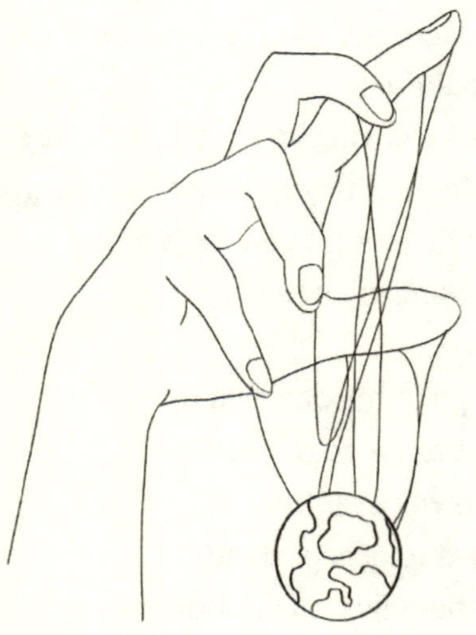

Sravanthi Tanakallu

Embrace Belonging

In search of belonging, the human race yearns,
Finding solace in family, where love is unconditional,
Embracing friendships and creating bonds, filling the air
with laughter,
Celebrating moments through communities we formed,
A shared identity from the nation that we belong,
United as one, on this vast planet we live on.
Yet questions arise, as doubts begin.
Do we truly belong in this vast cosmic sea?
Or are we lost souls, drifting and wandering free?
Even if we find our place, in relationships and ties,
What do we do with belonging?
Allowing greed and division,
We abuse the essence of our soul,
Forgetting compassion and love.
But let us not lose hope, for change is within our reach.
To mend the broken bonds,
We must embrace belonging with humility and grace,
Nurture the connections,
Making this world a better place.
There lies great potential in belonging,
In uplifting and inspiring.
Let empathy guide our steps,

as we walk this planet,
And rediscover the true worth of our collective birth.
So let us mend the fractures,
heal what has been broken,
Embrace belonging, as a chance to be reborn.

•••

Where Am I?

Where am I?
Standing at the edge of a double-sided sword-
Dreams that liberate and dreams that gives you scars,
Choice between right and wrong,
Paths that scare,
Paths that's uncomfortable,
Paths that maybe dangerous,
and paths that have lusty mirages with hidden knives.
I have always been presented with a choice between
dualities.
Should I consider my past to face my present situations?
Should I look into my uncertain future that is fearsome?
Because they say this moment is all you have got to live.
And this moment is just tearing me apart,
Trying to collect the pieces to stick them together,
But clearly, it's not happening.

Life and it's Weird Ways

Life is so weird, I think sometimes.
What do we think?
What are we looking for in this chaotic world?
How do we feel different emotions?
Happy one moment, sad the next.
How do we meet people?
How do they become strangers to friends?
How do we start, and how things change along the way?
We are so much similar, yet we are so different in many ways.
Our thinking patterns, our fears, our issues, our relationships with one another.
Everything is same, but so different
What makes us all?
What runs deep down in each one of us that is common?
What unites us?
What is this all about?
Life and its weird ways!

Sravanthi Tanakallu

In the Middle of a Storm

In the middle of the flow,
Waiting for the storm to pass,
Finding my way
And paths.
Walking away,
I will return one day,
Not the same,
Not the same.

Sravanthi Tanakallu

Just Breathe

Hold on for a little longer; it's going to be great.
I know it's suffocating; just try to breathe.
Just breathe..
Just breathe..
As long as you can breathe, things are going to be okay
again
Remember, you came a long way already, and don't give
up, just before reaching the finish line
It's going to be alright and it's going to be amazing
For I'm not sure what I'm or where I'm heading towards..
One thing for sure, to find it out, I need to breathe
Just breathe..
Just breathe..
One step at a time
One step at a time
And miles to go, before I stop!

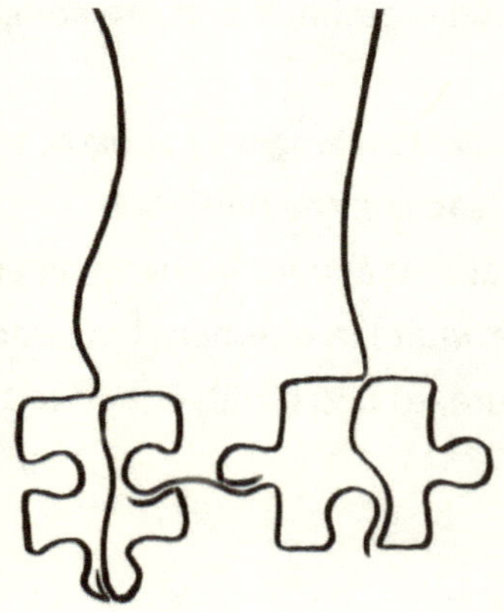

Sravanthi Tanakallu

Life is a Puzzle

Life is like a puzzle.
When you start, you don't know where to begin.
So You pick a piece, place it somewhere, then pick some more,
And Try to fit them
In the process,
You may choose wrong pieces many times,
No matter how many pieces you pick,
They won't fit where they don't belong.
As they have their own place.
But when you finish, you see what a beautiful picture you've created.
Every piece falls into place.
And there is no right or a wrong piece,
As each one completes the whole,
And together, they make a beautiful and perfect picture.

Sravanthi Tanakallu

Be True to Yourself!

What's good and what's bad, who can say?
Who decides and who judges, anyway?
Who's watching, who's checking?
And who holds the guide, by the way?
When they're just as unsure as you!
If only you knew, it's all circumstantial,
And everything changes,
Even for you.
Then the only truth you need to know is—
Be true to yourself!

Wise Words from a Friend

Someone once told me,
"Trusting isn't wrong,
But cheating is."

• • •

Sravanthi Tanakallu

Tears

Tears rolled from my eyes,
Nonstop,
as I waited,
Hoping they'd understand me.
There were times I had so much to share,
But felt unsafe,
Unsure,
Uncomfortable.
Each time, it felt like a weight on my chest,
A hurt in my stomach,
Pain in my heart,
And sadness stuck in my throat.
My eyes filled with tears,
Ready to roll down my cheeks,
To release the pain,
To let it out.
I'd hide sometimes,
Wanting to cry in secret,
So they wouldn't see my pain,
Wouldn't know how deeply it hurt,
Or that I longed to express what I felt.
I wanted to avoid them,
So I wouldn't have to explain.
And so, most times, I chose to cry alone—

Behind closed doors,
Under my blanket,
Late at night,
When the world was quiet,
And I was safe to feel the pain.
But in those moments of tears,
There was a beautiful release.
Crying out from the depth of my pain,
With folded hands,
Surrendering to something bigger,
Asking for help,
For strength to face it all.
I felt safe then,
Letting it all go,
Not holding back,
Showing my vulnerability.
In those moments,
I felt heard,
I felt seen.

•••

Sravanthi Tanakallu

Hustlers of Life

In the rush of life
Trying to be someone,
Trying to become something,
You forget to slow down,
To sit,
To breathe,
To do what you enjoy,
And avoid what you don't.
But no, you can't stop.
You have to keep going,
Keep doing,
Be this,
Be that.
Otherwise, you're losing,
Falling behind.
But wait—
What am I really losing?
Where am I going?
Who am I competing with?
What am I trying to achieve?
And at what cost?
I'm not sure.
Everyone is hustling,
So I feel I need to as well,

Between Shadows and Sunlight

To stay in the race,
Or I'll be left behind.
This fear,
It takes away the meaning of life.
Chasing after things that aren't real,
Running a race that never ends.
I'm missing out on
The simple joys.
Because simple seems boring now.
I have too many options for everything—
From food, to clothes, to places, and more.
So many choices,
And it makes me want to keep searching for more.
Things get boring too quickly,
Too easily.
I won't stop.
I need instant satisfaction,
Everything right at my doorstep,
Like quick Maggi noodles in two minutes.
Even faster is better,
Because then I can look for something else,
And then something after that.
I've gotten used to this.
Slowing down feels painful.
Having no choice feels dull.
This is my life now.
I don't know how to stop,
And I don't want to know.

Because it's easier to indulge.
Everyone else is doing it,
So why question it?
Just follow the crowd,
And keep hustling!

Letter to My Younger Self

Hello Kid,
How are you?
I'm sorry for what you're going through right now, but remember this:
You are not what others say you are.
Don't let those comparisons get to you.
Their thoughts come from their own beliefs, fears, and doubts.
You don't have to believe them, because that's not who you are.
I want to remind you:
You are beautiful, and you are enough just as you are.
You deserve all the good things in life.
There's a bright future ahead for you, and you don't need to be afraid or doubt yourself.
You are capable of amazing things.
From where I am, I know that:
You'll grow bold, free, creative, funny, smart, and independent.
You will travel the world, volunteer and be very confident.
You'll change careers and inspire others.
And people will love you for being yourself.
So don't let what people say define you right now.

Their words reflect their own fears and limits, not who you
are.
You are enough, just as you are.
And I'm always here to support you, love you, and be with
you every step of the way.
Love you!

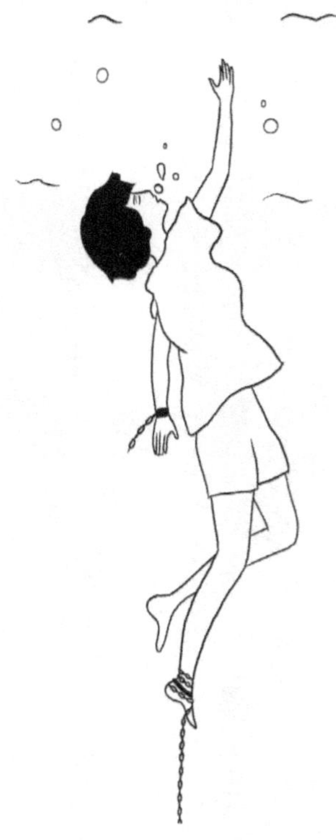

Sravanthi Tanakallu

Words

Words spoken in anger,
In frustration and in pain,
They linger for so long sometimes
And they hurt you more than we realise,
Leaving deep scars inside.
So the words you said still hurt me,
And they stayed while I tried to heal.
Knowing how words can hurt,
I can't give you that pain.
So I chose to be kind today,
To listen and to care
I know you spoke in anger,
But your words felt heavy,
Like a weight on my chest.
You may not have seen my pain,
And maybe you didn't understand.
If only you knew how much it hurts,
Maybe you wouldn't have said what you did.
I can't blame you for being unaware,
But I hope you think before you speak,
So you don't hurt someone else
With words that can't be taken back.
But I'll keep being kind and strong,
Not because I don't have anything to say

But today I choose kindness over anything
And today I chose to break the cycle
Because words have more power than we think.
And I use them to make people not break them.

●●●

Sravanthi Tanakallu

Universe and it's Magic

The universe puts you in situations when you're ready,
When it knows you're strong enough to handle them,
When it knows you're meant for it,
And when the time has come.
So I was placed in the middle of some heavy pain,
Pain I thought I couldn't bear,
Feelings that felt overwhelming,
Emotions I couldn't unravel.
But it was a do-or-die situation,
Either face it or have it forced upon me.
At first, I resisted,
But then I slowly gave in to its magic,
I began to trust,
Gradually learning to let it be.
It's still painful,
But now I know it's helping me open up.
It's like peeling off the layers,
To find the treasure within.
Those emotions have become simpler,
Pain no longer feels so hurtful,
It's just an emotion peeling away,
Revealing my true gift.
By not running from it,
By sitting with it and feeling it,

I've grown and will be growing!
I'm deeply grateful for this moment.
I can see the sunshine just beyond,
It's there!
Of course, with all these blessings, it has to be.

Between Shadows and Sunlight

I've grown and will be growing!
I'm deeply grateful for this moment.
I can see the sunshine just beyond,

Reflections

How do you see your own journey of personal growth and self-discovery reflected in the themes of the ‹growing’ section?

____

____

____

____

____

____

____

____

____

____

____

____

What specific moments or images in the ‹growing’ section resonate with your own experiences of growth and self-discovery?

____

____

____

____

____

____

____

____

____

____

____

____

How do the above poems in the ‹growing› section inspire you to approach your own challenges with resilience and hope?

____

____

____

____

____

____

____

____

In what ways does the ‹growing› section encourage you to embrace both the light and dark moments in your life?

How can the reflections in the ‹growing› section help you find meaning and purpose in your everyday experiences?

Notes:

Healing

Woods

The thing I love about woods is,
It really pushes you
out of your comfort zone.
Lets you Acknowledge your fears
Slowly Overcome them
Accept the unknown,
Let go of the unwanted
Nurture yourself
Live slow
Enjoy boredom.
Live with less.
Learn to survive.
Experience little things,
Be a part of nature.
Coexisting with Animals,
Waking up to Sunrises,
Sunsets that complete your day.
Colors of nature.
And this abundance,
You learn to Share,
Care.

Live a little more,
And love a lot more.
And you realise you are really never alone.
In this wild wild space,
With innumerable possibilities!

Sravanthi Tanakallu

Conversations with Ocean - Part 1

Dear Ocean,
How have you been?
Been a while since we met!
Did you miss me and our conversations?
But I certainly did!
You look gorgeous as usual
Acha, tell me one thing
How can you look so magical and calming?
Do you meditate?
Is that your secret now?
Why are you silent this time?
I'm waiting for your answers;
I want to know it all.
Yeah I get it, I'm being impatient right now.
But what to do!
I have so many questions,
And I thought at least you answer.

Patience dear friend, Ocean says!
With a gentle hug of waves.
Sun is about to rise in sometime;
Look around you carefully

Those golden rays,
The waves and the reflections,
The birds,
My depths,
Everything that's inside those depths!
My very own existence,
And its formation,
The rivers that travel miles to become one with me,
Letting go of their fear of unknown,
Letting go of their ego and
Losing their identity;
To become a part of something spectacular and
magnificent.
Each of them makes me look beautiful!

Me: What can I say, my friend!
I didn't realise how much I missed you until this moment.
You surprise me every time.
Thank you for the conversation today!
I love you a little more each time!

See you soon.
Your dear friend by the beach.

• • •

I Pray

Folding my hands
I pray!!
To surrender.
To make me an instrument of hope, compassion and peace.
To follow the path of righteousness.
To give strength to face adversities.
To have the courage to fight my fears.
Bless me that I seek,
To love than to be loved,
To give more than to receive,
To understand more than to be understood.
For it is in loving that we receive love,
It is in sharing that we prosper,
It is in forgiving that we are forgiven,
It is the ending that leads to a new start.

Fleeting Moment

Sky stretching vast and endless
Painting the canvas with its blue hues
Clouds use the canvas as a stage to dance,
With its graceful moves and forms, their dance has no end
Telling stories through their patterns silently
Trees join this Symphony of motion,
With a Soothing breeze,
Rustling leaves,
And birds chirping in distance,
Completing the masterpiece
A show beyond compare!
My heart skipped a beat
Witnessing its divine performance
Getting lost in this grandness
Time stands still
A fleeting moment of joy and wonder

In Search of You!

In search of you
I walked
With hope and love in my heart
Leaving behind,
Family, Friends and foes
Attachments
And any worldly possessions that I had

Then I reached a land with no human
In the lap of mother nature
I let go of my ego
Lived a slow and simple life
Waiting to find you
I walked and walked
Passing through
hills and forests
Mountains and deserts
I had no strength in me
To walk anymore

Then a river found me
Gave me a ride
We sailed and sailed
Till we reached the ocean

She taught me to have patience
Let go of my fears
And just flow with it
Days and months passed
But there's no you anywhere
Then the wind offered to help
He landed me over the clouds
I flew with the birds miles
Sang with them your favourite music
They taught me freedom
Gave me company till I reached the stars

Stars shined brightest that night
Moon light lit the entire universe
They are the sweetest
They taught me to love unconditionally
Shared their secrets with me
And about this magical land
Where everyone found what they are looking for
So I got ready with eagerness
That I'm finally going to see you
They gave me a twinkle to wear
So I looked pretty when I found you

Here I'm
In this magical land
Where everything felt like one
They breathe in sync

Between Shadows and Sunlight

Dance and sing together
Even though they are different
But they are one
I can feel you around
But I cannot see you
Then there was a voice, asking "how was your journey?"
It was yours
I know that voice
Heard it million times before
And strangely
You know every detail of my journey
Without me telling you
How did that happen?
You even know the secrets shared by the stars
Only if you were with me, you would know that

Then I realised,
He was with me throughout
Walking each step with me
Holding my hands
Laughing and Crying sitting next to me
Help me let go
Teaching me along the way
You are in the journey with me, to find you
Present there in those moments
And there is no you separately
Only if we have the heart to look for you
We will be able to find you

You are present everywhere
And in everyone
All the time
All the time

Conversations with Ocean - Part 2

Dear Ocean,

Sitting right here at the beach
Looking at you,
I wonder,
How is it for you right there?
In those depths, where sun rays won't reach & it's dark
and cold, you have so many secrets!
Filled with fossils, fascinating creatures, life thrives and it's
beyond beautiful, I'm sure.
But does it get overwhelming with everything or do you
feel the burden of those storms?
Life is different by the beach.
Moment to moment!
But you give me inspiration.
I always feel, you are so powerful, those depths remind
me of the depths of my soul.
You always remind me to reconnect with my being and to
feel the beauty of it.
My heart is experiencing the ups and downs of life, just
like the waves of the ocean.

So much is happening inside you and yet from here you look so spectacular, powerful, thriving and calm.
My heart fills with so much gratitude every time I meet you.
I'm happy, grounded and alive mostly.
I will come again sometime soon to play with the waves and sit calmly hearing the sounds of the waves, watching you and wondering what's there in those depths.
Next time teach me a little more about you and in turn about myself.

Your's
Loving friend by the beach

I Wanna Fly

In despair I looked outside my window, unable to move my
body
I see a bird flying high above the clouds
I followed that without realising
She took me through the curves of the green mountains
Then I saw a beautiful river flowing through
I felt the presence of the wind on my face
I smiled and looked down and I see houses with people
Then suddenly I realised that i'm that bird and I love flying
high above
And far from everything
I loved flying and flew as far as I could go
Exploring my heart out
I felt alive doing that again and again
Now each time, I look at that window, I wanna fly
I see the bird and we fly together
Until it's dark and we had to get back to our little nests

Many Souls Hidden in One

We are many souls hidden in one!
Try new things without fear
It blows your mind what's there inside you
Some you love
Some you hate
But every part has something to offer you

• • •

You Are the Hero in Your Story

Every soul you meet in this life has a role to play,
Your parents, chosen by you in some way,
With their thoughts, patterns, and lineage.
They shape the life that you're meant to lead.
Friends you encounter, relationships too,
Each has a purpose, a part just for you.
This is your show, your story to steer,
They play their roles, then they disappear.
You are the hero,
The lead in your story,
There is no good or bad story to tell,
So direct the way you want it to be,
Experience it fully, from moment to moment.
Learn from each one of it,
Let yourself grow,
That's all that's expected,
That's all there is,
And that's all you need to know.

Balance

We are here in this moment,
but we won't be here forever.
While we are here,
we must navigate the dualities of life:
Love and hate,
laughter and tears,
light and darkness,
kindness and ruthlessness,
right and wrong,
left and right,
poverty and wealth,
life and death.
One cannot exist without the other;
It is the essence of our existence.
They help us learn and grow
True balance is found only between these opposites.

Sravanthi Tanakallu

Surrender

Growing up, I believed in God—mostly out of fear.
Then, over time, that belief faded.
I looked around and saw others getting through life so
easily,
while I had to fight, chase, and struggle,
and even then, it felt like nothing came easy.
Eventually, I stopped praying, frustrated and angry.
I kept asking, Why me? What did I do wrong?
There were no answers, so I gave up.
Years went by.
One day, without seeking, without asking why—
I was just living, rebelling whenever I could.
And then, unexpectedly, a path appears.
I found myself wondering, You chose me again? But why?
I still didn't know, and I had more questions:
What's the plan this time?
Why not just give me the simple life I wanted?
But slowly, I realised,
maybe this is meant to help me grow,
to push me toward my fullest potential.
Like I am in the process of becoming the diamond
To be the best I can be,

To live a life that's truly worthy.
And so, I surrender to learn, to grow,
and embrace this path
even if I don't have all the answers.
All the time!

Where I Belong

I won't put myself in places
I don't belong
where I'm disrespected,
unwanted,
hurt,
held back,
surrounded by negativity
or undervalued.
I pray for the wisdom to recognise these places quickly
and the strength to leave.
As I belong where there's value, growth, strength, and
greatness.

Prayer - Part 1

In this borrowed time I have,
I pray to find the wisdom to live fully
To trust,
to be kind, honest,
to fill my life with love,
to spread joy,
to share and care,
to give and receive love.
To make memories,
to simply live,
to let go of anger, fear, doubt, and jealousy,
and to leave, when my time comes,
Without any attachment to this life!

Reminder to Myself

Hello Sunshine,
Don't be afraid to show your love today and every day.
You brought a smile to someone's face, made someone
feel loved and cared for, and truly listened.
You're remembered for all the kindness you share.
You make the world a better place.
So go ahead, spread love, share joy.
Someone out there needs it, and for them, you're the light
they need.

It All Begins with You

Everything you seek begins with you.
The respect you desire—offer it to yourself.
The compassion you crave—extend it inward first.
The love you give—make sure it reaches you too.
Before standing up for others, stand up for yourself.
You might want to give it all to others,
But if you don't provide it to yourself first,
How can you expect anyone else to offer it to you?
Perhaps, just perhaps, you need your own kindness more
than anyone else does.
And when you can genuinely give it to yourself,
Only then can you truly give to others.
Otherwise, you may unintentionally bring them down,
Causing more harm than good.

•••

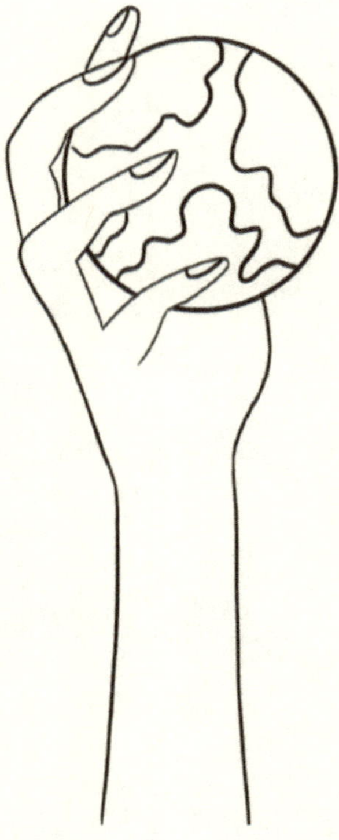

Sravanthi Tanakallu

My World

In my world, though not perfect, but it's kind,
Where peace fills every heart and mind.
People smile and greet with care,
Hugs are warm,
hands help each other,
We cheer and stand up for one another.
We sit and talk, not turn away,
Sharing love through what we say.
Kind words flow in every chat,
Love is the language we're good at.
Laughter is what we hear the most,
And we all toast to simple joys.
Yes, there are problems and tough days,
Worries and troubles come our way too.
But we know we can face it all,
Grateful, mindful, and standing tall.
We live in peace with soulful hearts,
In a world where kindness will never cease.

Sravanthi Tanakallu

Gratitude

At times, I might forget to see,
The many good things that are part of my life
Like parents who gave me the space to be free and bold
That friend who stayed through tough days
stranger I met in a cafe that I could trust
A random call, just checking in,
A message saying, "I love you"
The work I do which I feel passionate about,
Opportunities that came my way.
And those I lost,
though then unsure,
Now I see,
they had a purpose.

People who stayed,
and those who are gone,
That trip I could take,
Book I randomly found,
Smiles that made my day
unconditional love I felt
And Blessings received randomly
Each played their part as life moved on.

I questioned, not knowing what was true,
But now I see the path each one created.

A bigger story is yet to come,
Much greater than I thought,
As I wait for it to unfold,
I feel grateful, strong, and bold.
Each person, friend or foe,
Each experience, good or bad,
Each situation, big or small,
Makes me thankful,
makes me complete.
Every part of me feels this way,
Grateful now, and every day.

Light at the End

Some days I see no way forward,
but when I look back,
I wonder about all those paths that opened up.
Now, when things get tough,
I remind myself to have patience
and I know
I'm stepping forward to better times even on those bad
days

Being Human

I can't breathe,
I can't breathe,
I can't breathe..
Where are we heading towards as people, as society?
Too many layers, structures, systems and rules that only divides all of us into countless parts.
We are too complex, complicated, and crazy but we can definitely live in peace.
We must get back to being human, we have definitely lost it.
After all, being human is what we are meant to be in the first place.

Beauty in the Chaotic Wait!

We see some hard stops
And get worried
But some shine brighter and beautiful in those
So it's not the problem with the stops
It's how you see it.
Beauty in the chaotic wait!

Sravanthi Tanakallu

What Do You Want?

Heart wants love
Mind wants success, money
Soul wants peace
But with open wings, I will reach the sky
Where dreams and destinies lie.
Love, success and peace intertwine,
Guiding the spirit of mine.

Connection

In the spiral of thoughts,
Moments freeze,
as you stare into the abyss,
encountering a person within yourself.
Lines emerge,
connecting the depths of your inner journey with the
vastness of the universe.

• • •

Everything is Changing

It may seem nothing has changed
but the reality is, everything is changing with each passing
moment

Many Souls in One

We are many souls hidden in one!
Try new things without fear
It blows your mind what's there inside you
Some you love
Some you hate
But every part has something to offer you

•••

Thanks to Everyone Who Crossed My Path

To everyone who has crossed my path,
It's because of you that my journey unfolded the way it did.
Each of you, in your own way—big or small—
Has shaped my life, and for that, I am truly grateful.
May you find healing,
May you continue to grow,
And may your lives be filled with blessings and goodness.
Thank you to each and every one of you.
Sending only love and peace.

Reflections

How do the poems in the 'healing' section make you feel, and what memories do they bring to mind?

____

____

____

____

____

____

____

____

____

____

____

____

In what ways do the themes of resilience and self-discovery in the above section reflect your own life experiences?

____

____

Is there a specific poem in the 'healing' section that resonates with you deeply? What about it speaks to you?

What insights or lessons from the healing section can you apply to your own journey of growth and self-awareness?

How do the poems help you process your own experiences with love, loss, and personal growth?

Notes:

I am Peaceful

I am Grateful

I am Magical

Thank you for choosing to read ‹Between Shadows and Sunlight.’ I hope you found solace and inspiration through the journey of self-discovery, love, and healing. Your patience and support mean the world to me. I sincerely pray that you are blessed with beautiful things in your life, find the strength to navigate through tough times, experience unconditional love, heal, discover yourself, love yourself, and conquer the world. Thank you once again for being a part of my journey. May you shine through the shadows and sunlight, and grow into a beautiful human.

With so much of Gratitude,
Sravanthi Tanakallu

www.ingramcontent.com/pod-product-compliance
Lightning Source LLC
Chambersburg PA
CBHW031627170726
47990CB00017B/399